MW01296061

Bitcoin: Mastering Bitcoin & Cryptocurrency for Beginners

Bitcoin Basics, Bitcoin Stories, Dogecoin, Reinventing Money & Other Digital Currencies

2nd Edition

Table of Contents

Introduction

I want to thank you and congratulate you for downloading the book, "Bitcoin: Mastering Bitcoin & Cryptocurrency For Beginner".

This book contains proven steps and strategies on how to invest and mine cryptocurrencies.

With the sudden interest of the investing public on Bitcoins and other cryptocurrencies, it is important that these investors are given honest and accurate information about these digital currencies so that they can decide for themselves if they are willing to trade and mine such electronic currencies. This book provides mining information about Bitcoins, Litecoins, and Dogecoins. Bitcoin is considered the most popular and profitable among the different cryptocurrencies available in the market today. On the other hand, Litecoin is considered second in value and popularity. Dogecoin is relatively a new entrant in cryptocurrencies and holds a lot of promise.

This book also offers information about the most popular websites that a new investor can visit to acquire more information about cryptocurrencies. Such websites can be a huge help if the individual wants to be up-to-date with his knowledge about cryptocurrencies. Lastly, this book discusses the taxation issues currently facing the use of cryptocurrencies. Being relatively new, it is expected that governments are quite behind in regulating transactions involving cryptocurrencies. A new investor must know about such issues so that he can be prepared once governments provide taxation rules on cryptocurrency transactions.

I encourage you to share this book with your friends and family, and please take the time to write a short review on Amazon to share your thoughts.

Chapter 1: What is Cryptocurrency?

Cryptocurrency is virtual money. It is used as a medium of exchange in digital format. In 2009, Bitcoin, the first decentralized cryptocurrency to become popular, was introduced to the public. When it became popular, other cryptocurrencies followed suit. These other alternative currencies are commonly referred to as *altcoins*. In essence, a cryptocurrency includes the concepts of cryptography to an economy that is secure, decentralized, and distributed. Compared to fiat currency, it is not controlled by any government or financial entity. Each cryptocurrency has limited production that is predetermined and highly publicized.

There currently exist hundreds of specifications on cryptocurrency that have been determined, but a lot of these are based on Bitcoin. Within the cryptocurrency system, there exists a community of people who mutually distrust each other, known as miners. Miners ensure the balance, integrity, and safety of the cryptocurrency system. These miners are members of the general public and are tasked to protect the network. The basic assumption is that most of these miners are genuinely doing their best to keep the system secure since they are motivated by a financial incentive.

Although it is possible to avert the cryptocurrency's security, doing so can be very costly. Production of a particular cryptocurrency is limited and the introduction of new units is gradual. This strategy prevents hyperinflation and imitates the scarcity of precious metals. Therefore, hyperdeflation is experienced by the cryptocurrency as production reaches its limit and the cryptocurrency becomes highly popular. A cryptocurrency can't be seized by a law enforcer since no financial institution can lay hold of it and it does not exist physically like cash.

A cryptocurrency is digital money secured by cryptography in order to ensure transactions are safe and addition of currency units is tightly controlled. Unlike fiat money, it can't be easily counterfeited due to its security feature. It isn't issued by any financial authority, therefore it is impossible for any government to manipulate it. Because of its anonymous nature, transactions of the cryptocurrency can be used for tax evasion and money laundering.

Because of cryptocurrency, fund transfers are easier using private and public keys to ensure the security of the transaction. Transaction fees are minimal as compared to fees charged by financial institutions and banks.

However, cryptocurrencies are virtual and aren't stored in a central repository, which means that, when the computer crashes, the individual's cryptocurrency balance can be erased if the user didn't keep a backup. The value of a cryptocurrency is highly dependent on supply and demand. As such, the price can experience wide fluctuations.

Decentralization and Cryptocurrencies

A currency that is decentralized means that it is generated by the whole economic system communally, at a rate that is established during the creation of the system. This is unlike a centralized economic system, where governments and corporate boards are the only ones allowed to control how currency is supplied; how fiat money is printed and added to digital banking ledgers. Since governments are currently unable to produce cryptocurrency units themselves, they cannot back firms, entities, or banks that hold decentralized cryptocurrencies in the form of assets.

Proof-of-Work Codifications

This was the first timestamping codification invented. SHA-256 and scrypt are the most commonly used proof-of-work designs. Bitcoin uses SHA-256 while Litecoin uses scrypt. A proof-of-work scheme is actually a protocol to prevent denial of service attacks and other abuses like network spam which require processing time by a service requester or computer.

SHA-256 is actually part of the SHA-2 set, which consists of hash functions used in cryptography. The set was developed by the US National Security Agency and published as a US Federal Information Processing Standard by NIST in 2001. SHA means Secure Hash Algorithm. SHA-256 is a hash function in 32-bit words. The SHA-2 set is patented in the US but released as a royalty-free patent.

Scrypt, on the other hand, is a key derivation protocol that is password-based. Colin Percival developed scrypt for the purpose of online backup by Tarsnap. The algorithm makes it expensive to launch a large-scale hardware attack because it would require a huge amount of memory. It is used by cryptocurrencies like Dogecoin and Litecoin.

At the moment, scrypt is the dominant proof-of-work codification used in the cryptocurrency world. Other hashing algorithms for proof-of-work do exist, for example, CryptoNight, X11, SHA-3, and Blake.

Proof-of-Stake Codifications

A proof-of-stake scheme is a form of cryptocurrency security. The concept is based on coin age, which is the amount of currency multiplied by the time the currency is held. To generate a block, an individual sends money to himself in order to use up the coin age for a predetermined reward. A new block is generated for the user over time. This scheme secures the cryptocurrency network and also produces new units gradually without the need for more computational power.

Peercoin is known to use both proof-of-stake and proof-of-work schemes, but the main blockchain is determined by the proof-of-stake generation. According to Peercoin's developer, it is more difficult to attack the network through it.

Chapter 2: History of Cryptocurrency

There have been attempts to establish a cryptocurrency in the past. In 1998, an anonymous ecash system known as "b-money" was created by Wei Dai. Not long after that, Bit Gold was developed by Nick Szabo. Just like its future successor Bitcoin, the Bit Gold system made it necessary for users to perform a proof-of-work design, with the solutions being assembled and published cryptographically. Hal Finney later used the work done by Dai and Szabo to come up with a currency system that relied on reusable proof-of-work.

David Chaum of ecash and DigiCash tried to incorporate cryptography with digital money. However, it was only in 2009, with the introduction of Bitcoin, that cryptocurrency was recognized. Satoshi Nakamoto, a pseudonym, is widely recognized as the Bitcoin developer. This cryptocurrency makes use of SHA-256 in its proof-of-work design. Namecoin, Litecoin, Peercoin, and Freicoin soon followed. There are other cryptocurrencies that had been developed but they were not successful because they offered few innovations. During the first two years, these cryptocurrencies became popular. However, it was when the price of Bitcoin rapidly escalated in April 2013 that interest in cryptocurrencies started to rise rapidly.

How the Bitcoin Idea Was Birthed

To best understand Bitcoin, it is important to first grasp the idea behind its creation. When Satoshi Nakamoto created Bitcoin, he was attempting to develop a totally new method of paying for things online. The aim was to totally change the way the system worked because the current payment systems simply had too many flaws.

When the 2008 financial crisis hit, the whole world felt the effects of an economic meltdown. In fact, eight years later, some countries have not yet fully recovered from the drop in value of their fiat currency. When the world financial system was in a state of near-collapse, the majority of central banks decided to fall back on the only solution they knew – printing more money. They started printing more and more money, and simply flooded the markets with cash. The aim was to substantially cut interest rates so as to avoid another Great Depression scenario.

This led to wild instability of fiat currencies and led to some countries deliberately trying to devalue their currency so that their goods could become cheap and therefore more competitive in the global market. As usual, governments resorted to bailing out some banks using the extra printed money, thus making the fiat currency even more worthless.

In other words, debt from privately owned institutions was transferred to members of the public, therefore increasing the debt burden on future generations. Many people felt that this was unfair socially as well as economically. Nobody can really say how printing and flooding the market with more fiat money will affect an economy in the long run, but bankers were willing to ignore government regulations just to keep the system moving in the same direction.

This is where Bitcoin came in. Satoshi Nakamoto wanted a decentralized monetary system that could not be manipulated by a few powerful elite individuals. Nakamoto decided to create a financial system that would swoop in and disrupt the existing financial infrastructure. It is not clear if Bitcoin was designed to totally replace the existing monetary system. However, there are certain banks that seem impressed with Bitcoin. They are actively looking for ways to adopt its technology to suit their own purposes. Since Bitcoin runs on a blockchain, which is an open source technology, anyone can use it and build upon it. This means that Bitcoin can be described as more of a motivating ideology and not just an ordinary payment system. Its potential has not yet been fully cultivated. This can only happen over time. It may be hard to understand the entire concept of Bitcoin and the technology it uses. However, be open to the idea of how the technology can be adapted to resolve the existing financial needs.

The honest truth is that the global financial system as it exists currently is full of problems. Central banks have abused the system and everybody else had to pay for it. Even future generations will end up paying for it. Bitcoin could be one of the viable solutions available, or maybe it won't be. The biggest aspect about Bitcoin is decentralization. This means everyone shares in and contributes to the system. This is known as a peer-to-peer system, where everyone has an ownership stake in Bitcoins, not just governments or banks. Bitcoin is nothing without individual users, and the more users there are, the better. If Bitcoin is to succeed, more people have to be willing to use the payment system to trade and do business.

Criticism of Cryptocurrency

Cryptocurrencies can be very risky because these digital currencies are exposed to extreme volatility as well as to pump-and-dump schemes. There were cryptocurrencies that had been pre-mined, had very high rewards to the initial miners, or have mysterious launches. The cryptocurrency Ripple had been known to be pre-mined. There were also cryptocurrencies which were just duplicates of current cryptocurrencies with a few changes but nothing more to offer. Coinye West, a comedy cryptocurrency, had been ordered to cease-and-desist on January 7, 2014. Some cryptocurrencies can be exchanged for cash but a majority can only be exchanged for other digital currencies. Banks don't accept cryptocurrencies. In some cases, these financial institutions won't accept virtual-currency firms as clients. Financial regulators in many countries have also warned against cryptocurrencies, while there were others who took concrete steps to discourage the public from using the digital currencies.

It is possible to lose cryptocurrency permanently from your computer hard drive. This can be due to data loss or malware. Once cryptocurrency is lost, it is gone forever from the market. Not many merchants currently accept cryptocurrency as a means of payment. The numbers are increasing, but until the required criteria are reached, cryptocurrency cannot be considered mainstream.

It costs a lot of money for new miners to join cryptocurrency pools. There is a lot of technological advancement happening within cryptocurrencies, and new miners must have specialized software and hardware. Cryptocurrency has also been criticized for being non-reversible. Once a couple of blocks approve the transaction, it is done. There is no form of consumer protection, for example, a credit card chargeback. If Bitcoins are stolen or lost, there is no institution to complain to.

Chapter 3: Bitcoin as a Cryptocurrency Standard

As a decentralized currency, Bitcoin makes use of peer-to-peer mechanics in order for verification, transaction processing, and currency issuance to be collectively implemented by the cryptocurrency network. It is free from any government's interference or manipulation. However, there is also no central figure that ensures smooth operation and supports Bitcoin's value. Bitcoin is mined using computers that solve difficult algorithms as well as crunch numbers. It has a maximum predetermined production of 21 million. The rate of production is pegged at 25 Bitcoins per 10 minutes. By 2140, it is expected that the maximum Bitcoin production would have been reached.

Bitcoin differs from fiat money. The latter is backed by a government and supervised by the country's central bank. Theoretically, fiat money has no maximum production limit. Bank deposits of the currency are insured by the government in cases of bank failures. On the other hand, Bitcoin isn't supported by any central bank or government. Its value is determined by the present market value. Furthermore, if a Bitcoin exchange closes shop, users can no longer retrieve their Bitcoin balances from it.

Because of transaction anonymity and decentralization, Bitcoin is also used by criminals in weapons procurement, smuggling, drug peddling, and money laundering, which prompted the US Department of Homeland Security, Federal Bureau of Investigation, Securities and

Exchange Commission, and the Financial Crimes Enforcement Network to monitor and sanction cryptocurrencies. The Financial Crimes Enforcement Network has defined cryptocurrency administrators and exchanges as businesses, thereby including them in government regulation as of March 2013. The Department of Homeland Security froze Mt. Gox's account due to allegations of money laundering in May 2013. The Department of Financial Services of New York subpoenaed 22 payment companies that handled Bitcoin to inquire about the firms' measures to ensure consumer rights are protected and money laundering is prevented.

The Technological Aspects of Bitcoin

For a peer-to-peer payment system to be credible, the technology that runs it must be considerably powerful. As a digital currency standard, Bitcoin is very powerful. There is a lot of emphasis going into turning its blockchain technology into a tool that the financial industry can use.

Bitcoin technology provides numerous technological options, yet most of its potential still remains untapped. There have been a number of attempts made by different platforms to increase the accessibility and usability of Bitcoin. Unfortunately, there have been setbacks in terms of security. Bitcoin is not yet the finished article, but as people learn better ways to utilize it, improvements will take place.

Most of the people who seem very interested in Bitcoin technology are financial industry players. They are attracted to the great potential of its open ledger system. Open ledger means that anybody with an Internet connection can view real-time financial transactions taking place within the network. This is an advantage because it makes it easy to track several things at once.

Bitcoin is designed to bypass the present world financial system. It has the potential of providing services to people who do not currently have any or total access to bank accounts. In the West, having a bank account is no big deal, but in the developing world, it is still a challenge for many. Credit and debit cards are slowly replacing cash as currency. In many developing countries, mobile payments are widely available. Now that Bitcoin is offered on mobile payment platforms, it can easily be the payment method of choice for the under-banked and unbanked.

Even unbanked consumers who live in regions with limited Internet coverage can use Bitcoins. There are certain services that exchange Bitcoins for text messages that are sent to any mobile phone number. This would allow people with no access to the Internet to still acquire Bitcoins for transactions. One of the greatest technological aspects of Bitcoin is its network. Every transaction in the Bitcoin system is recorded and tracked in real time. Users can simply log into the network and take a look at global financial data from anywhere in the world. A user can also monitor the real-time movement of their payment as it travels throughout the system. This is only possible due to the blockchain system that Bitcoin uses. If the present world financial system adopts such kind of transparency and openness, everyone would benefit.

As a cryptocurrency standard, Bitcoin still has room to maneuver. It is easy to set up a Bitcoin payment option on your website, but using it in real stores is different. There are some payment processors who can help in converting Bitcoin transactions to hard cash. The good thing about accepting Bitcoin as a currency is that bank payments are received quickly, usually within 24 hours. The transaction fees are also quite low.

Using Bitcoin as Currency

One of the most talked about aspects of Bitcoin is its price. At the time of writing this book, the price of one Bitcoin was $619. Bitcoin has seen a steady climb in price since its creation. This price depends on its users and follows the law of supply and demand. Currently, the demand isn't that big, but time will tell how this might change.

Though Bitcoin is acceptable virtually as well as in the real world, it is still not considered real currency. This is because a payment system must meet specific criteria to be considered a currency. In order for Bitcoin to become accepted as currency, it must be more widely used. Sellers have to be convinced to accept Bitcoins as payment for goods and services. This is quite difficult, but more difficult than this is convincing consumers to use Bitcoins. There is no point setting up a Bitcoin payment system in your store if no consumer wants to use it.

Bitcoin fits the bill for a digital currency. No matter where a person is in the world, Bitcoin is accepted as a means of digital payment. It is possible to exchange it into any other local physical currency in the world. There are no transaction fees and payments are received quickly.

Benefits of Bitcoin to Retailers

It doesn't take much investment to start using Bitcoins as a retailer. It can coexist together with the normal payment system. All you need is an Internet connection. There are certain advantages a retailer gets when using Bitcoin as a payment system. As already mentioned, the transaction fees are low and payments are deposited in the bank account within one business day. Some payment processors charge a very small margin to change Bitcoins into local currency.

Unlike cash, which is calculated to the second digit, the value of a Bitcoin is calculated to eight decimal points. For example, you can sell a product for 39.98765432 BTC. This can help a retailer to price his products more accurately.

Since Bitcoins are acceptable as a form of digital payment all over the world, a retailer has a very large potential consumer base. This means there is no need to offer a wide variety of different currencies if you accept Bitcoins. In fact, accepting Bitcoins as payment and then buying goods using the same Bitcoins ensures that transactions maintain their value. Converting to a local currency usually, leads to some loss in value.

Benefits of Bitcoins to Consumers

For consumers, Bitcoins make buying goods and services easier. There is no need to carry around notes and heavy coins in your wallet. Since Bitcoins uses a decentralized system, payments can be made to anybody at any time, whether it's a holiday or a weekend. Processing of online digital payments is also done quickly.

The Anonymity of Bitcoin

It is not really clear if Bitcoin is anonymous or not. Using digital currency does not give users total anonymity, but there is a certain level of anonymity it provides. The anonymity of Bitcoin comes from the use of a wallet address. Wallet addresses are letters and numbers that are combined to form a string of text that hides the identity and location of a user. While many other digital payment methods do not provide such anonymity, Bitcoin is able to protect users to a certain degree.

Since Bitcoin wallet addresses are contained in an open ledger, all incoming and outgoing transactions can be monitored at any time. Though it is not possible to know who owns the sending and receiving wallet addresses, a user can be able to see the amounts transacted. It is then possible to go to www.blockchain.info and monitor a specific wallet address. A person will be able to view current transactions as well as past ones. Since all transactions linked to a particular wallet address are public knowledge, real anonymity on the Bitcoin network is not possible. However, if Bitcoins are being exchanged for fiat currency, there is a bit more anonymity. Someone may see the Bitcoins being transferred to the exchange's wallet address, but where those Bitcoins go after that is unknown.

Using 3rd Party Anonymity

There are some ways to stay anonymous while using the Bitcoin system. Such methods are still being refined and do not tend to be user-friendly. The truth is that most people who insist on being completely anonymous are usually trying to conceal their illegal activities, for example, tax avoidance or smuggling illegal merchandise. Using 3rd party technology to stay anonymous involves mixing Bitcoins together in one wallet address and then removing them from a totally different address. This breaks the link between two addresses.

There is the risk of losing Bitcoins by using 3rd parties. It is always advisable to conduct research on any external service provider who offers anonymous Bitcoin transactions. Digital currencies were designed to lock out middlemen so that users could always retain control of their money. Hiring a 3rd party is not what Bitcoin is about. It may even raise a red flag about the activities a user is engaging in. In reality, most regular Bitcoin users do not care much about staying anonymous anyway.

Privacy Protection

The process of protecting your privacy while transferring money using Bitcoin is not straightforward. There has to be some prior planning. One way of ensuring privacy protection is to generate a fresh wallet address every time a new transaction is conducted. If a user is sending funds to your address, you have the option of asking them to send the Bitcoins to a newly generated wallet address that is not directly linked to your existing one. This new address is established with the sole aim of receiving funds for only one transaction. After the funds have been transferred, the address is never used again. This enables a user to isolate their individual transactions. This is considered the first measure when trying to protect user privacy.

Another way to ensure some sort of privacy is to create *change* addresses. This precaution is dependent on the mode of storage of a user's funds – the type of operating system the computer runs on and the Bitcoin client being used. If a user installs the Bitcoin Core client on their computer, they will be able to generate a fresh change address whenever they send funds to another Bitcoin user. A change address is used when a user has a certain number of Bitcoins in their wallet but want to send less than that balance. Obviously, there will be some change left over in the wallet after the transaction. If the user has installed Bitcoin Core client, they will be able to send the remaining funds or "change" to a freshly generated account. This breaks the link between the original wallet address and the new one. However, someone can still retrace the steps the funds went through by examining the blockchain.

It is also possible to maintain user privacy on the Bitcoin network by simply avoiding the tendency to post your Bitcoin wallet address in a public place. Some users sometimes place their wallet address on their blog or website. This can compromise security. In case someone comes across the public wallet address and is able to link it to a specific user, the user's privacy will no longer be guaranteed.

Chapter 4: Alternatives to Bitcoin

Litecoin

Litecoin can be considered to be Bitcoin's biggest competitor when it comes to the digital market currency. A very strong contender to beat Bitcoin, Litecoin processes small transactions faster than Bitcoin. Introduced in October 2011, founder Charles Lee likened Litecoin to silver if Bitcoin is gold. What sets Litecoin apart from Bitcoin is the fact that Litecoin mining uses ordinary desktop computers, unlike Bitcoin mining, which requires high-powered computers. A regular user cannot mine for Bitcoins on their average home computer, but mining Litecoins is very much possible using a home CPU. The upper production limit of Litecoin is 84 million while Bitcoin's limit is 21 million. Its processing is also faster compared to the blockchain; 4 times faster than Bitcoin's at 2.5 minutes. A miner is able to earn about 50 new Litecoins for every block.

Though it was created to work just like Bitcoin, Litecoin's major difference is in the fact that it uses an open-source program. This essentially makes the Litecoin network more secure. Litecoin uses Scrypt proof-of-work while Bitcoin uses SHA-256. Scrypt as an algorithm incorporates SHA-256, but the calculations it produces are much more serialized. Although the shorter processing time doesn't bring about greater benefits, the use of Scrypt does. Scrypt doesn't use ASICs, which are responsible for increased efficiency and mining power. The introduction of ASICs chips has greatly increased the difficulties of entering Bitcoin mining. Litecoin is very similar to Bitcoin so the former's developers had little to explain about it. The timing of the introduction of Litecoin was also great. Miners who had been left out by ASICs shifted to Litecoin mining without any additional investment in hardware. Currently, Litecoin is cheaper than Bitcoin.

Ripple

Introduced by OpenCoin, ripple is similar to Bitcoin because it is both a payment system and a currency. Chris Larsen established the company in 2012. However, the idea of Ripple is actually much older than Bitcoin. In 2004, Ryan Fugger had an idea to design a decentralized monetary system that would allow people to create their own money. Ripple's currency component has a similar math foundation as Bitcoin, while the payment system ensures fund transfers to another entity within seconds as long as the transfer is within the Ripple network. Prominent companies like The Bitcoin Opportunity Fund, Lightspeed Venture, Andreessen Horowitz, and Google Ventures have investments in ripple. A lot of people, however, are confused because it doesn't directly compete with Bitcoin. Ripple complements other fiat and virtual currencies by offering a decentralized exchange and payment system.

The core mechanism that Ripple uses to monitor balances is similar to what Bitcoin offers – wallet addresses, private and public keys. A user can use the same public and private keys to sign messages and transactions in both the Ripple and Bitcoin networks. On the other hand, Ripple does not use a proof of work algorithm and there is no mining involved on its network. This lack of mining is responsible for the quick deflationary nature of Ripple. Ripple uses a ledger chain that shows a transaction tree of all the transactions that has occurred since the previous ledger. Unlike Bitcoin that has a fixed number of currency units at its upper limit, Ripple has a maximum number of currency units of 100 billion, and these units then immediately start to permanently reduce as more transaction fees are paid.

Technically, Ripple is an Internet protocol which can act as conduit for data and websites in a standard way. It can process payments regardless of the financial institution or provider used as long as the transaction makes use of the ripple protocol. Actually, ripple is a currency, a distributed exchange, and a payment network.

MintChip

MintChip is created by the Royal Canadian Mint. It acts like a smartcard that can hold digital value, which can be transferred to another smartcard. It is similar to Bitcoin. There is no need for a personal identification. However, MintChip is supported by the Canadian dollar. The digital currency was announced in 2012 and a contest was launched for users to think of ways on how to use the MintChip. The chip is secure and can be used with an SD card so that it can be connected to mobile devices and computers. A private key is used with the smart card to sign transactions. A user needs the receiver's ID if he wants to send payment using MintChip. David Everett, a British expert in cryptography, is considered MintChip's technical architect.

Peercoin

Considered a clone of Bitcoin, Peercoin has few differences with the popular cryptocurrency. It has no maximum production limit and is developed to reach an inflation rate of 1%. Theoretically, this can boost the longevity of Peercoin. This cryptocurrency is mined the same way as Bitcoin. It uses the proof-of-work protocol. However, the plan is to eventually move it to proof-of-stake. The Peercoin algorithm is based on the size of the user's holdings.

In order to mine Peercoins, the user has to spend his holdings depending on the combined coin age of his inventory. When the user mines Peercoins, he resets the age if his holdings. The advantage of this system is that it minimizes energy waste. It also makes it more expensive to launch the "51% attack" to destroy the system. Transaction fees are lower because it offers a better fee structure.

However, Peercoin still mimics the way Bitcoin is mined. It also uses ASICs. But, once it moves to the new mining protocol, it can be environment friendly to use it.

Namecoin

Namecoin offers functionality in managing information access. Although it can be used as mode of payment, it is more like a distributed DNS (Domain Name System). It is ICANN's peer-to-peer version. For 0.01 Namecoin, a domain name can be registered and maintained in a blockchain. If the user transfers the rights of the domain name, a fresh construction can occur. The advantage of Namecoin is that it curtails Internet censorship. It also minimizes downtimes. However, cybersquatting can be a problem because domains can't be seized and are inexpensive. Namecoin can also manage decentralized email, torrent attackers, and logins. Because of this feature, it is expected to thrive if Bitcoin collapses.

Primecoin

Bitcoin mining is an energy waster. As such, waste increases as Bitcoin grows. Primecoin implements proof-of-work scientifically. Instead of providing a solution to arbitrary hash, miners of Primecoin look for prime number chains. New blocks are found every minute thereby hastening transaction times as well as smoothing difficulty adjustments. Primecoin is self-adjusting and tries to mimic gold. The disadvantage in using Primecoin is that, when interest in the cryptocurrency increases, more miners become interested in mining because of the price increases. As more miners mine Primecoin, production is reduced because the difficulty level of Primecoin mining also increases. The demand can be greater than the supply, which encourages price volatility.

Dogecoin

Dogecoin is derived from Litecoin and showcases a Shiba Inu on the logo. Just recently introduced in December 2013, its initial production is quite fast, unlike other digital currencies. Before 2014 ends, a total of 100 billion Dogecoins are expected to be circulated. For the succeeding years after 2014, it expected to produce 5.2 billion Dogecoins yearly. Even while Dogecoin isn't as popular as the other cryptocurrencies, it is being widely used in online tipping.

Billy Markus, an ex-IBM engineer is credited to be the creator of Dogecoin. However, it was his friend, Jackson Palmer, who conceived the Dogecoin idea. Because it is a spawn of Litecoin, Dogecoin also uses Scrypt, which doesn't require specialized hardware to mine the cryptocurrency.

There are online exchanges that offer DOGE/LTE and DOGE/BTC trading. However, only Bter offers DOGE/CNY trading. Early in 2014, AltQuick.co also started offering DOGE/USD trading. By the end of January 2014, Vault of Satoshi exchange started offering DOGE/CAD and DOGE/USD trading. Dogecoin uses a public key cryptography to create both a public and private cryptograohic key. A private key can decode a public key. This means that a Dogecoin owner can distribute his public key to anyone without fear that it can access the Dogecoin information. The public key is distributed openly because it is the address the user can use to receive Dogecoins from other users. However, the private key that can access the Dogecoin in the address must be kept secure and safe.

Dash (Darkcoin)

Dash is a peer-to-peer cryptocurrency that was created in January 2014. Originally, it was known as XCoin (XCO) but it then changed to Darkcoin a month later. In March 2015, Darkcoin became known as Dash. The network uses an open source system and provides users with instant transactions, private transactions, and a form of token fungibility.

Dash offers users a high level of decentralization and it also uses a proof-of-work codification. It is supported by a chained hashing algorithm known as X11, which was developed by Evan Duffield. Unlike the other forms of cryptocurrency that rely on either SHA-256 or Scrypt, Dash utilizes 11 rounds of various hashing functions. These 11 cryptographic hashing algorithms ensure that coins are processed and distributed in a fair manner. Since the network runs on chained hashing algorithms, the average return of a high-end CPU is the same as that of a GPU. This algorithm also ensures that the electrical power used by the GPU is around 30% less than what Scrypt uses. The computer system is also maintained at a temperature that is 50% cooler. This is an advantage for miners, as they do not have to contend with high energy bills and excessive stress on their computers. Dash is currently considered to be among the 7 most widely used cryptocurrencies.

FeatherCoin

Feathercoin is generally referred to as Litecoin's Litecoin. This is because it is to Litecoin what Litecoin is to Bitcoin. The maximum number of Feathercoins is about 25 million, which is four times more than Litecoins. Feathercoin is not a new altcoin. It precedes most of the other digital currencies. However, it has never done much to distinguish itself.

Feathercoin processes transactions faster than Bitcoin and is extremely abundant in circulation in comparison. It can be used to buy certain things. It is not a fully decentralized digital currency, and it makes use of "Advanced Checkpointing." Most users consider Feathercoin to be a speculative altcoin with little future promise.

Quarkcoin

As a digital currency, Quarkcoin has earned a bad reputation in the past. It has been linked to pre-mining and pump n' dump schemes. It uses a special 6-way hashing algorithm that makes it very secure and a strong alternative to Bitcoin and Litecoin. The hashing algorithms are meant to protect Quarkcoin from attacks while also preventing the use of special hardware to mine it. Quarkcoin has a proof-of-work algorithm that is more complex than Bitcoin. While Bitcoin has a block interval of 10 minutes, Quarkcoin is much faster. It has a block interval of a mere 30 seconds. However, despite some of its advantages over Bitcoin, Quarkcoin still has a lot of challenges to overcome.

WorldCoin

This cryptocurrency doesn't offer much to users to set it apart from the other digital currencies. The only advantage it has over Bitcoin is that it has short transaction times – a claim of 30 seconds per transactions. It is not yet that popular with users, though it is very attractively branded. It is more of a speculative coin, and most Bitcoiners refer to WorldCoin as a "scamcoin," – a pump n' dump scheme that doesn't really distinguish itself or offer anything special to users. It has a maximum predetermined production of about 34 million coins.

CasinoCoin

CasinoCoin was formally launched in July 2013. It is a decentralized cryptocurrency that was created to help gamers access their favorite online casino games. CasinoCoin acts like a universal casino chip that can be transferred between different online casino gaming exchanges and applications. This makes the digital currency independent of any platform.

This particular peer-to-peer open-source digital currency does not have any value on its own. It only becomes worth something when playing games on online casino platforms. On the exchange market, CasinoCoin can be traded in for other cryptocurrencies like Bitcoin. It can also be exchanged for fiat currencies. Casinocoin uses a Scrypt proof-of-work protocol. It has a total coin number of about 336 million coins, with 50 coins being assigned to every block. There is no pre-mining with CasionCoin. It is as secure as Bitcoin, as accessible as Litecoin, as abundant as Feathercoin, and as fast as Dogecoin. Though it can be considered a general purpose cryptocurrency, it is primarily used for online casino gaming.

StartCOIN

This cryptocurrency is a bit different from the rest. It is a digital currency that is used as a reward for people who support projects that bring change to their communities and society. The more a user supports, pledges, and shares information about a change project, the more StartCOINS they receive. It is a cryptocurrency that is designed to support and promote crowdfunding for good causes.

Like Dash, StartCOIN uses the X11 proof-of-work protocol. The maximum number of currency units for StartCOIN is 84 million coins. 50% of StartCOINs have already been pre-mined. 90% of the mined StartCOINS are donated to initiatives and active StartJOIN users. The block reward is halved after every 12 months.

To get involved, a user has to register on the StartJOIN website and become part of the crowdfunding community that leverages social media to spread the message of change.

NXT

This is both a cryptocurrency as well as a payment network. NXT, also referred to as Nxtcoin, was released by the anonymous software developer BCNext in November 2013. Unlike some of the other cryptocurrencies, NXT does not require mining and uses the proof-of-stake protocol to achieve a consensus for transactions. The rate of creating a block is about one minute. NXT was created to act as a platform for building other financial services and applications. Users of NXT are allowed to create new currencies inside the existing system, running the risk of devaluing the currency itself.

As software, NXT is very complicated infrastructure that carries a lot of risks. However, this means that external services can be built on top of its blockchain. For example, external developers can add enhancements or features to improve the usability of the system. The blockchain is written entirely from scratch and is coded using Java. It uses a standard client that stores keys in the form of a unique passphrase rather than storing them in a wallet file. This makes it easier to access using any kind of NXT software.

The way NXT verifies transactions is dependent on the size of the stake a user owns. The larger the stake a user owns, the greater the chance to add a block to the chain. These block authors are always chosen at random.

Chapter 5: The Future of Cryptocurrencies

Each cryptocurrency has its own limitations. Usually, the problem of cryptocurrencies arises when a computer crashes and the owner doesn't have a backup. This means that the user's holdings are wiped out. A cryptocurrency is also exposed to hacking, although it is widely believed that such limitations can be overcome by technological advances over time. The most pressing problem of a cryptocurrency is government scrutiny and regulation. As a cryptocurrency becomes popular, governments and financial regulators become increasingly interested in controlling it.

Although more and more merchants are willing to accept cryptocurrencies, only a small portion of the global population uses them. For these digital currencies to succeed, more and more consumers must be encouraged to use them. A stumbling block to their use is their complexity, which is only understood by users who have the technological understanding of cryptocurrencies. If a cryptocurrency is to be successful, its mathematical formula must be easy to understand yet difficult for hackers and scammers to attack. It must protect and safeguard the consumers while ensuring decentralization. It must deter money laundering, tax evasion, and fraudulent activities while preserving user anonymity.

Chapter 6: Developing Trust in Bitcoin

Before a cryptocurrency gains acceptance and momentum within the community of users, people must first trust the idea. This is one of the most difficult things for a digital currency to achieve the moment it is launched. When it comes to Bitcoin, this trust has to work both ways – both the users and the network have to trust each other. A user is always in control of their funds, but this does not mean they have total control over the Bitcoin network. A user has to believe that they will not wake up one day and find the network gone and their money disappeared.

Most Bitcoin supporters would argue that there is very little chance of this happening. On the other hand, there is only one thing in life that is certain – there are no certainties! One feature that enhances people's trust in the Bitcoin network is the fact that there are a lot of individual users and Bitcoin nodes. The function of the nodes is to make sure that the Bitcoin network is always running.

The idea of Bitcoin is built around the concept of decentralization. Most users have a hard time trusting this idea. Bitcoin is not controlled by any one person, so a failure in one part would not be catastrophic to the entire system. This means that one person or a small group of people would not be able to take down the system. The only way to shut down the whole system would be to bring together a super-large group of users to put in a massive effort, which is next to impossible.

Decentralization also causes distrust because there is no central authority to complain to in case things go wrong. The Bitcoin network is just a bunch of individual users. In case a user loses all or some of their Bitcoins for some strange reason, there is no recourse, and nobody to reimburse the lost funds.

Developing Trust in the Technology

Bitcoin is usually compared to the Internet during its early days. Not many people accepted the service because they didn't think it was necessary or useful to their everyday lives. It is human nature to reject change, especially if the problem being solved is not something the majority of people think about. However, today things are much different. The Internet is something that people need every day, regardless of geographical location. Getting people to trust a technology and transition into it can be very difficult.

The same principle applies to Bitcoin. Getting people to see the need for the technology and trust in it is going to take a long while. Though Bitcoin is engaging in a number of platforms and projects, it has still not penetrated into the mainstream. People need to be educated more about how Bitcoin works and what it is designed to do. This will help them understand its utility and benefits in everyday life.

This is not to say that Bitcoin is not trusted at the moment. There are quite a substantial number of people who trust the technology. It provides a cheap way to send money to anyone anywhere in the world. Bitcoin technology may be seen as a small-time player by the major financial players, but it may soon give them a run for their money.

Developing Trust in the Currency

Bitcoin is not really a currency since it does not meet certain criteria or bear features of a conventional currency. It is more of a digital payment solution. However, quite a number of merchants have decided to trust in Bitcoin as a payment system, and use it together with other traditional modes of payment. As a currency, Bitcoin does not cost merchants anything if they chose to accept it as payment. There is also no extra infrastructure that needs to be set up.

A merchant can integrate the Bitcoin system into their physical as well as online shop. Converting Bitcoins into local currency is a fast process. For consumers who are interested in using Bitcoins to purchase goods and services, it allows them to transact without cash, debit, or credit cards. Of course, to obtain Bitcoins, consumers first have to get their hands on this digital cryptocurrency. This is possible through buying Bitcoins or earning them some other way.

What makes most people distrust Bitcoin as a currency is the fact that an individual has to take responsibility for their funds at all times. People are scared of this aspect because they are used to having a large institution taking care of everything for them. People love to cede control of their funds to banks or the government. They do not want this kind of responsibility because it seems to require too much time and effort. Trusting Bitcoin as a currency means investing time to take control of your funds every time.

The Risk and Volatility of Bitcoin

Just like every other currency or payment method, Bitcoin comes with risks. The difference is that the risks Bitcoin carries are not the same as other currencies. Due to its blockchain technology, Bitcoin does not bear risks like chargebacks or fraud, which plague traditional currencies. There is a lot of transparency and transaction charges are quite low compared to wire transfers or credit cards. On the other hand, Bitcoin is still a relatively new technology that is an ideological payment method. It is still being developed and enhanced for consumer use. This makes investing in Bitcoin a risky venture.

Bitcoin's blockchain technology is developing rapidly and has great potential for growth. It will also create jobs for people in the future. At the end of the day, investing in any Bitcoin venture carries the same risks as any other conventional startup. Speculating on Bitcoin prices, however, is a different matter altogether. This is not a good idea because the price has shown rather sharp fluctuations in the past. Bitcoin's price is very volatile and as an investment vehicle, it is risky.

There are a lot of investors who call Bitcoin "fake internet money." This has not prevented many others from buying Bitcoins and storing them. Investors feel that BTC is a better way to transfer or store value compared to other existing methods.

Chapter 7: Investing in Cryptocurrencies

An individual who wants to invest in cryptocurrency must treat it the same way as he would treat other investments, which are highly speculative. This means that the investor must know that he faces the risk of losing everything, primarily because a cryptocurrency has no intrinsic value. The price of the cryptocurrency can experience large price swings thereby increasing the investor's risk of loss.

How to Start Investing

It is important to practice due diligence prior to investing in any cryptocurrency. An investor must do his research and try to learn about the cryptocurrency first. There are various sources of online information like chat rooms, websites, comparison sites, forums, block chains, and mining pool sites. A prospective investor must learn about volatility, trading volume, trading difficulty, trading value, and coins per day. It is also important to learn about the reputation of the cryptocurrency developer, mining algorithms, forked block chains, age, attacks, pre-mines, and events as well as news that can affect the trading of the cryptocurrency. It is possible for the would-be investor to reduce risks if he exerts effort in learning about the digital currency. After researching the cryptocurrency, the new investor must draft a trading plan that must be followed in order to reduce the risk of losses. It is something that is unique to the individual because the plan depends on his trading goals and style. In choosing a cryptocurrency to invest in, he must also be able to monitor volatility. If there is no trading volume in his chosen cryptocurrency, there won't be any movement on the price. If there is no movement on the price, there's no way to profit from trading the electronic currency.

The cryptocurrency exchanges that have higher volumes also have more volatility. The price of the digital currency in higher volume exchanges can differ from those lower volume exchanges. Thus, it is good practice to look for an exchange with the volatility and volume that fits the investor's trading style.

Using Charts

Charts are an important aspect of cryptocurrency trading. They are also the most overlooked. For this type of trading, the 1 year and 6 months charts are significant, as these charts help the investor recognize long-term trends. The exponential moving average chart is a good tool that indicates if the trend is up for correction. If there's a significant divergence from the upward trend, it means the price of the cryptocurrency can move downwards. As such, the investor can't take a long-term position.

On a shorter term, cryptocurrency trading can be riskier because there are short reversals that slow down the downward movement of the price. An investor can take advantage of such short reversals to gain on short-term trading. Scalping, shorting, and flipping are very risky. However, it is possible to gain profit using these strategies by paying close attention to trends, moving average convergence divergence, and orders. In buying a position, it is best to enter when the price has dipped. It is important to ensure that the interval is commensurate to the length of term the investor wants to keep the holdings. A short-term investor can consider the hourly dip in price while the long-term investor considers the weekly or monthly price dip. Once the position has been taken, he must monitor the news, orders, and trends to help him decide what to do next.

Charts provide important evidence to show the worth of a cryptocurrency at a particular time. Trends are culled from these charts. Through trends, the investor can learn about value cycles, which he can use in maximizing profit and minimizing risks. Chart overlaying is a smart strategy employed by a lot of investors. An investor can overlay a past chart with a new one when a trend or pattern emerges. If the patterns agree with each other, the old chart can be used to predict the outcome of the current trend.

Identifying Patterns

Patterns can be double bottoms, double tops, and head and shoulders. These patterns are used to predict reversals of a particular trend. The triple bottoms and triple tops also indicate strong trend reversals. In these patterns, a new price moves toward the opposite direction of the present trend and confirms the beginning of a change in the present trend. The triangle is also another easy to spot and popular pattern. In this pattern, the price of the cryptocurrency moves to form a triangle. When pattern cycles go lower than the previous one, it is possible for a downtrend to emerge, which signals the investor to consider stop loss or shorting. An ascending triangle, on the other hand, occurs when the pattern cycles go higher than the previous one. This indicates an uptrend and signals an investor to make margins or accumulate profits. A cup and handle pattern is often used for long-term trading. A cup pattern occurs when there's a pause in an uptrend. It often indicates sideways trading. The handle is formed when there's a slight correction.

The lines in the exponential moving average chart are very important in short-term trading because they easily react to information and data thereby forming a trend. The direction of the lines often indicates the direction of the price of the cryptocurrency. The moving average convergence divergence, on the other hand, is a simple tool used in cryptocurrency trading. A positive difference between the short-term and long-term moving average indicates an uptrend while a downtrend is imminent when the difference is negative. The Golden Cross pattern is formed when the short-term average crosses the long-term average in an upward direction. On a short-term trading, this uptrend is expected not to last when there's a quick and intense divergence of the averages.

Diversification in Cryptocurrency Trading

All investors are warned against putting all their eggs in one basket. They are highly encouraged to diversify their investments. They must continuously search for other schemes to include in their portfolio so that when one investment fails there are other investments that can act as safety nets.

The pump and dump scheme is rather old, and is often used by investors who sell or flip large volumes of cryptocurrency at the best possible price. Some scheming investors often encourage new investors to do the same so that the price of the cryptocurrency will rise. When the value reaches their targeted margin, they often exit their positions, leaving the others empty-handed. This scheme hurts the cryptocurrency and is often labeled as a scam.

Pre-mined cryptocurrencies must be avoided because developers often just want to cash in on their gains quickly. It is also good practice to be wary of manipulated or attacked exchanges. In most cases, investors are often stuck when the site is down for long periods or when there are cases of thefts. Chat rooms can be very good sources of trading information. However, the investor must be careful about the lies and fluff because scammers just want to profit from the ignorance of new investors. It is still best to stick to the investor's trading plan.

Chapter 8: Bitcoin Wallets

A wallet is an application that is stored on a computer hard drive and is used to hold a user's Bitcoins. When this software wallet is installed, it creates a wallet.dat file to hold personal data. A Bitcoin software wallet can be obtained from Bitcoin.org website. The software for Bitcoin wallet is open source, thus guaranteeing transparency and security.

Syncing a Bitcoin Wallet

Syncing a Bitcoin wallet involves refreshing and updating the software so that the account information provided is up-to-date. The syncing process is dependent on the type of device being used, so it's important to first find out how to do this. Another thing to remember is that when the wallet is closed or the computer shuts down, the wallet needs to be synced again.

Backing Up a Bitcoin Wallet

Every new Bitcoin wallet that is created needs to be backed up within the software. The backup file can also be saved on an external hard drive or a flash disk. Since the file is encrypted, it will provide the safety and assurance that in case something happens to the computer, the user will still be able to access their Bitcoins.

Understanding Bitcoin Addresses

A Bitcoin address works just like an email address. They are both designed to send and receive data. However, there is one major distinguishing feature between the two. A user can own as many

Bitcoin addresses as possible, with all of them being used to send and receive funds. It is usually recommended that a user on the Bitcoin network use a new Bitcoin address every time they undertake a transaction. Though there is no technical issue with using the same wallet address for every transaction, a change in address ensures an added layer of protection. This may prove too cumbersome for some users, and the decision will be influenced by the number of transactions that a person processes in a day.

Generating a new address is not complex, and furthermore, a user does not need to be connected to the Internet. The process is free and is done through the Bitcoin software. Alternatively, a new address can be acquired from an online wallet provider or an exchange. A Bitcoin address is composed of between 26 and 35 characters containing both letters and numerals. A Bitcoin address usually starts with either a 1 or a 3 and is case sensitive. Any deviation from the sequence of numbers and letters invalidates the recipient's address, thus preventing the transaction from going through.

Keeping the Bitcoin Wallet Secure

A Bitcoin wallet should always be closely guarded, just as one would a real wallet or a debit card PIN. The Bitcoin Core client software enables users to encrypt their password. This prevents unauthorized access to a user's Bitcoin wallet in case heir hard drive is stolen. It is always a good idea to set a memorable password since the software will always prompt the user whenever they are sending funds from their wallet.

Securing Mobile Wallets

A mobile wallet can be installed on a Smartphone or a tablet, making it very convenient for use. These mobile devices are usually close to the user at all times and can be carried around easily. While both desktop and mobile Bitcoin wallets send and receive transactions via an Internet connection, the mobile version can still work without it. The mobile wallet is actually designed to send and receive Bitcoins through a Bluetooth Low Energy connection. It is this kind of versatility that has made Bitcoin popular and loved by users.

A mobile wallet is secured using a private key that is stored within the mobile device. The private key is what allows a user to access and spend their funds. To prevent funds from being misused or stolen by someone who borrows a user's phone, the mobile wallet requires a PIN code. This PIN code is four to six digits long, and after a certain number of failed attempts to give the correct PIN, the wallet is automatically locked. The owner of the wallet is then informed through email or SMS and provided with information on how to unlock the wallet.

Though storing the private key on a mobile device is a great security measure, there is some risk involved. Technology and consumer preferences are always evolving fast, with mobile devices being replaced every day. It is thus important to create a backup the moment the mobile Bitcoin wallet is installed. The software for the mobile wallet contains an inbuilt backup feature. The backup copy can be sent to a user's email or exported to Google Drive or Dropbox.

Securing a mobile wallet is the responsibility of the user. The aspect of decentralization gives full control for every process to the user. If a user is careless with their mobile device or does not backup their private key, restoring access to the wallet is impossible.

Securing Online Wallets

When Satoshi Nakamoto developed Bitcoin, he wanted to create a society where individuals interacted and transacted directly with each other, with no middleman involved. An online Bitcoin wallet is a banking service provided by a 3rd party. The service controls the user's funds, allows them to transact, a well as check their balance when they wish. The user essentially puts their trust in a 3rd party service rather than take control of their own funds.

The risks of using an online Bitcoin wallet service are tremendous and supersede the potential benefits. A user has to rely on the service provider to be honest at all times. Furthermore, though the user accesses their funds via a PIN, it is the service provider that owns the private key to the account. If the online wallet service is hacked or shut down, the user is powerless to access their funds. The online wallet platform provides options for additional security. However, no system is impenetrable, and the risk of hacking is always real.

Bitcoin is all about an individual taking responsibility for their personal funds rather than relying on another financial institution. An online Bitcoin wallet does not subscribe to the concept that Nakamoto for Bitcoin.

Securing Paper Wallets

A paper Bitcoin wallet is a document that contains the data required to create private keys. The paper wallet also serves the purpose of storing funds securely. The funds are stored in form of redeemable codes linked to a specific Bitcoin wallet address and can be used when purchasing items. For security purposes, a paper wallet should be used only once, since it is not designed for everyday use. The paper wallet can act as a gift for friends or family or as a tip to someone else. However, the recipient of the paper wallet must have their own Bitcoin wallet in order to import the private key linked to the address.

A paper Bitcoin wallet has certain advantages over the other forms of wallets. An Internet connection is not required, it cannot be hacked, and it doesn't depend on a 3rd party. However, it can be stolen, burned, lost, or damaged by water. The only way to keep it safe is to store it in a safe deposit box. This is not really practical for the majority of Bitcoin users.

Chapter 9: Understanding Bitcoin Transactions

For a Bitcoin transaction to take place, one user has to give another user a certain number of BTCs. This transaction has to be validated, meaning that there must be at least one input. This input is simply a reference to the output of a past transaction. A user must understand that each input in a Bitcoin transaction must be the funds that were unspent during a past output. Each and every input has to be digitally signed via the private key linked to a particular Bitcoin address.

Bitcoin payments are generally denominated in terms of satoshi, which is the smallest increment of a Bitcoin transaction. Satoshi are the eight decimal points that come after the period. Bitcoin is designed to be more divisible than traditional currencies, and a satoshi can be worthless today but very valuable tomorrow.

There are a number of methods a person can use to send Bitcoins to another user. The sender can simply ask the recipient for their Bitcoin address and remit the funds via the Bitcoin software. The recipient can also choose to send over a QR code, which the sender scans. All forms of Bitcoin software give users the option of creating their own QR codes. This code is embedded with the recipient's wallet address as well as the number of BTCs to be sent. For example, assume a user has received 10 BTC over the last one month and wants to send 4 BTC to another user. This transaction will generate one input, which is the previously received 10 BTC, and two outputs. Output #1 will be the 4

BTC being sent to the other user, while output #2 will be the unspent amount (6 BTC) that returns to the sender's wallet address.

Confirmations

In the Bitcoin network, every 10 minutes sees one new block being created and added. This occurs during the mining process. The function of a block in a blockchain is to verify and record any new transactions that take place. Once this happens, the transaction is considered confirmed. For example, if user A sends funds to user B, the transaction stays unconfirmed till a new block is created. As soon as the block is added to the blockchain, the new transaction is checked and recorded in the block. This is counted as one confirmation. Every 10 minutes after this, a new block is added, and these new blocks reconfirm the transaction within the network. Though certain services only need a single confirmation, most Bitcoin companies require six confirmations, which takes around 60 minutes. The reason for requiring so many confirmations is to reduce the chances of a payment being annulled.

There are instances where a transaction takes place but it fails to be confirmed as soon as the next block is created. This can be the result of two things. The first reason is that the transaction is fraudulent. If the signature of the transaction fails to match with its corresponding key, the network will reject the transaction. The second reason is that the person sending funds didn't send enough miners fee. A transaction with a very low miners fee may take a very long to confirm or will be dropped from the network.

Double-spending

A double-spend can be defined as a form of network attack where a specific set of Bitcoins is spent in multiple transactions. There are generally three major ways that a user can launch a double-spend. The first technique is to send two different transactions within the network in quick succession. This is known as a *race attack*. The person receiving the funds can prevent this form of attack by waiting for one of the transactions to be confirmed first.

The second technique is to pre-mine a single transaction into a block, spend the same funds, and then release the block so as to annul the transaction. This is known as a *Finney attack*. The merchant can avoid damage from a Finney attack by waiting for six confirmations for a transaction. If it is a small transaction, the number of confirmations required can be less, but at least one confirmation will ensure the transaction is secure.

The third technique for an attack is where a user takes control of more than half of the entire computing power of the Bitcoin network. This makes it possible for the attacker to reverse whichever transaction they want, as well as which transactions appear in a block. This is known as a *51% attack*. Such an attack can cripple the whole system. However, it is a rare form of double-spend and usually, doesn't target individual users.

Bitcoin Transaction Fees

It is important to understand that though Bitcoin as a worldwide payment network is considered to be free, this is not entirely true. For someone who receives Bitcoins from another user within the network, no transaction fees are involved. However, there are certain instances where transaction fees come into play. If a user wants to speed up their transaction, they have the option of including a minimal transaction fee. Many Bitcoin wallets offer users such an option. The fee ensures that the transaction is prioritized by including it in the next block available.

Those transactions with no fees are usually not prioritized. There are particular transactions that will be prioritized even if no fee is included. The user must be using a Bitcoin Core client, the transaction must be less than 1000 bytes, have outputs of 0.01 BTC and above, and of a high priority. If all these conditions are met, the transaction will be exempted from all fees. It is important to understand that every network block has about 50,000 bytes of unused space primarily to cater for such high priority transactions. The majority of Bitcoin transactions are about 500 bytes to 600 bytes.

Failure to meet these conditions attracts a standard fee of 0.0001 BTC for every 1000 bytes. The Bitcoin Core client system always prompts the user to either accept or reject the transaction fee. If the user opts to reject the fee, the transaction will not be prioritized, and the network will apply the confirmation slowly.

Chapter 10: The Profitability of Mining Cryptocurrencies

It gets more difficult to mine Bitcoins as time goes by. A lot of miners troop to the stores to buy the latest computer hardware to mine Bitcoins. However, with increased mining difficulty, a lot of miners are frustrated. At the rate things are going, a miner who begins mining only now won't break even. Thus, miners look to other cryptocurrencies to make a profit. In a report by coinwarz.com, they can make profit in mining other cryptocurrencies. Newegg and Amazon have reported they are out of stock for efficient mining tools. The AMD GPUs have gained resale values and people are buying them with the hope of mining cryptocurrencies before any release of scrypt ASICs is made.

Cryptocurrencies are exchanged for Bitcoins through various exchanges like cryptsy.com and bter.com. In cryptsy.com, the site has a feature that automatically sells any new cryptocurrency for Bitcoins. A lot of individuals find this strategy more profitable. However, it should be noted that miners still stick with Bitcoin mining because they trust the digital currency. They speculate that Bitcoin will grow in value, especially when Bitcoin becomes more secured and stable. There are also individuals who mine cryptocurrencies not for profit. They believe that the cryptocurrency will be accepted as a reserve currency globally. As long as there are people who believe in cryptocurrency, mining will still be profitable.

Being the most valuable of all existing cryptocurrencies today, the Bitcoin is peer-to-peer and decentralized. It doesn't need a clearing house or central bank to confirm the transaction. Because of the anonymity and security that Bitcoin offers, there are a growing number of individuals who prefer paying in Bitcoins. Compared to fiat currency, Bitcoin transactions are free except when the digital currency is converted to fiat money. To own a Bitcoin, a person has to mine it using a computer algorithm and hardware. A Bitcoin is unlocked each time a block of code is broken down. Even a fraction of a Bitcoin can be earned and traded.

Cryptocurrencies have limited production, therefore, there is no inflation or devaluation. As such, a lot of people are encouraged to have these digital currencies in their possession. Due to the difficulty in mining Bitcoins, it is no longer as profitable as before. The costs of electricity and hardware are also rising. Currently, speculators cause the artificial inflation of the Bitcoin. However, cryptocurrencies possess value.

Cryptocurrency mining requires an individual to invest on computer hardware. It is possible to start mining using cheap machines. However, that machine will be underpowered because mining requires the right graphics cards for GPU horsepower. Bitcoin mining now requires some specific ASICs like Butterfly Labs ASICs and TerraMiner. These ASIC miners can cost at least a thousand dollars. Other cryptocurrencies don't require special hardware. Most miners of other digital currencies trade their holdings for Bitcoins.

Chapter 11: The Problems With Cryptocurrency Mining

The main problem with cryptocurrency is that it fluctuates in value, which affects the payback rate of mining it. The price of Bitcoin had crashed, which prompted a lot of miners to abandon their mining efforts because the earnings they receive from Bitcoin mining aren't even enough to pay the electricity bills. Each cryptocurrency has its own payback rate primarily because each of them commands its own price. The payback rate is important because it determines if the mining opportunity is profitable or not, although there are individuals who stick to mining cryptocurrencies with the hope of eventually earning back their initial investments. Today, Bitcoin mining requires a huge investment in computer hardware. It doesn't make sense joining the pool of miners now because it won't be profitable anymore.

Another drawback to cryptocurrency mining is that users have to ensure their holdings are secured. Cryptocurrencies aren't controlled by any central bank, thus it is the responsibility of each user to be accountable for his cryptocurrencies. If the computer crashes, the user must have his own backup to ensure that his holdings are safe and secure. Hacking and theft are also problems that a user must face with cryptocurrency mining. Because of its anonymity, it becomes impossible for anyone to track any attacks on the cryptocurrency.

Chapter 12: Bitcoin Mining

Bitcoin mining is the process of creating additional Bitcoins to the Bitcoin currency system. These additional Bitcoins come into existence through a decentralized computational process that involves solving complex mathematical equations. A Bitcoin miner needs to have hardware that is dedicated and designed for such a process, as the mining can take place at any time of day. A miner not only works to generate more coins for use in the network but also secures the Bitcoin network by confirming the authenticity of transactions. This verification is accomplished by running SHA-256 double round hash validation processes. Bitcoin mining speed is measured in hashes per second.

There are the five key steps in the Bitcoin mining process:
1. The user (or miner) works to verify if transactions taking place within the Bitcoin network are valid.
2. The miner bundles transactions into a block.
3. The header of the newest block is selected and inserted into the same block but in the form of a hash.
4. The complex Proof of Work problem is solved.
5. When the miner finally solves the mathematical problem, they add the new block to the local blockchain. The new block is then sent into the network.

The network rewards those miners who worked to release a block by giving them Bitcoins. This is compensation for contributing computational power. Those miners who dedicate more computing power get a larger share of the reward, which can be in terms of newly issued Bitcoins or transaction fees.

How to Start Mining Bitcoins

Step #1: Get the best mining hardware

Anyone who wants to become a Bitcoin miner must first procure mining hardware. When Bitcoin was first released, mining could be done with a regular computer CPU or even a high-speed video processor card. Today, this simply will not work. There are custom Bitcoin ASIC chips that are designed to perform at 100x the capability of the previous systems. Any individual who tries to mine with hardware that is less powerful than the ASIC chip will discover that they are spending more on electricity than they are earning from mining. It is important to buy hardware that is specifically designed to mine for Bitcoins. This can be done either on Amazon or through other 3rd party websites.

Step #2: Download the mining software

There is a special program that has to be downloaded before a user can begin mining for Bitcoins. There are a number of software programs that are designed for Bitcoin mining. However, the two most widely used are BFGminer and CGminer. These are command-line software and are preferred by advanced users.

If the person isn't technologically adept, he may have a difficult time setting up mining software. GUIMiner has been introduced to solve the frustrations of these average users. Once downloaded, the individual will be asked to provide some information like username, dot, worker ID, and password. If the individual is a Mac user, he can use Astroid. He can start Bitcoin mining once he has set up the mining software.

Step #3: Join a Mining Pool

With the increased difficulty in mining Bitcoins, a new miner is encouraged to join a mining pool, a group of miners who combine their computers' power to mine Bitcoins. A pool provides an easier and smaller algorithm for a person's computer such that, when combined with the work of other computers, will make it possible to solve the more difficult and larger algorithm. If a person decides to mine for Bitcoins as an individual, it may take them more than a year to earn any Bitcoins. The individual can earn Bitcoins based on his contributions to the pool. In essence, a mining pool provides consistent means of earning Bitcoins. Examples of pools to join include Slush Pool, Eligius, CK Pool, and BitMinter.

Step #4: Get a Wallet

The final step is to set up an online wallet, which is a repository of a person's Bitcoin holdings. A Bitcoin client can be downloaded from www.Bitcoin.org and installed to the individual's computer. A blockchain will be downloaded which can occupy as much as 6GB of hard disk space. If the computer has space limitations, a DVD can be ordered which contains the blockchain. A wallet address can then be created after installing the client. It is important to have a backup of the wallet.dat file on a separate device such as a thumb drive. If possible, a copy of the wallet can be printed and kept securely in a safe place. The backup is needed so that the individual doesn't lose his Bitcoins if his computer crashes.

Mining Difficulty

To make sure that the number of coins created daily does not exceed the set limit, Bitcoin mining is linked to a difficulty value. Mining difficulty is defined as the measure of the difficulty of finding a hash below the target value during the Proof of Work process. This is explained in the steps below:

1. More miners join the network and start mining for Bitcoins.
2. The rate at which blocks are created goes up.
3. The average time it takes to mine one block decreases. The Bitcoin network has an established average mining time of 10 minutes for every block.
4. As the mining, time reduces the difficulty rating increases so as to compensate.
5. The rate of creating new blocks goes back down.
6. The average mining time achieves a balance and goes back to normal. In case there are any blocks that are released into the network by fraudulent miners that fail to satisfy the required difficulty rating, the rest of the miners simply reject the block. It then becomes worthless.
7. Back to step 1.

Bitcoin Mining With ASICs

Bitcoin mining with ASICs is very much the same as mining with GPUs. It follows the same procedures discussed previously. The main difference lies in the use of mining software. BFG Miner is mining software that supports ASIC. The GUIMiner discussed earlier only supports GPUs. The software needs to be downloaded and installed on the computer. The ASIC must be connected to the computer. Once the software has been installed, it will ask for some information like mining pool, username, and password. The software will start mining once the setup is completed.

Cloud Mining

Cloud mining, also known as cloud hashing, is where a person purchases the capacity of mining hardware from a data center. Instead of a user buying their own personal hardware, they simply pay to use the hardware of a data center. Bitcoin cloud mining helps people generate Bitcoins without having to face any hardware, software, bandwidth, electricity, or other challenges. The mining is accomplished via a cloud, and users avoid the usual hassles related to heat, hosting, electricity, installation, and maintenance problems.

Benefits of Bitcoin Cloud Mining

1. The user does not have to deal with issues regarding generation of excessive heat.
2. The mining process is a quiet one because there aren't any computer fans humming loudly in the background.
3. The user does not have to pay high electricity costs.
4. In case mining of Bitcoins is not profitable anymore, a person does not get stuck with any mining equipment.
5. There is no hot equipment to create ventilation problems.

6. Some Bitcoin mining equipment companies may deliver preordered hardware late. With cloud mining, there is no reason to worry over delayed deliveries.

Disadvantages of Bitcoin Cloud Mining

1. It becomes difficult to verify some Bitcoin cloud mining operations.

2. The risk of fraud is high as there are some cloud mining companies that run scams.

3. Cloud mining is not as fun as creating your personal Bitcoin hashing systems.

4. Paying for cloud services eats into the user's profits. The cloud mining company may charge high fees due to expenses.

5. Some mining contracts may include cessation of payouts or operations in the event that the price of Bitcoins drops too low.

6. The user does not own the mining hardware.

7. The user does not have the ability to decide which software to use and cannot change what is offered.

Cloud Mining Cons

Prior to purchasing any Bitcoin mining contracts from a cloud service, a person must ensure that they are dealing with a legitimate business. There have been cases where Bitcoin users have been scammed by Bitcoin cloud mining services. Some just cease payouts all of a sudden, while others have been Ponzi schemes.

Different Types of Mining Pools

In a mining pool, the members combine their resources to distribute hashing power. However, rewards are also distributed equally to members depending on their contributions to solve a block. The individual must present a genuine proof-of-work that their resources solved to be eligible to receive the reward.

Pay Per Share

This approach provides guaranteed and instant payout for every share solved by a Bitcoin miner. Payment comes from the current pool's balance. It can be withdrawn immediately. Pay per share eliminates the difference in payment for the different miners. Most of the risks are transferred to the operator of the pool.

Proportional

This approach provides for an equitable distribution of the reward generated when a block is mined successfully.

Pay Per Last N Shares

This approach is the same as the proportional approach. The difference lies in the choice of shares as basis for the reward. The proportional method considers the round's shares while this approach considers the last N shares.

Double Geometric Method

This approach is a hybrid method wherein the operator assumes some of the risk. Using this method, the operator receives some of the payouts for short rounds. However, for longer rounds, the operator returns what he received.

Shared Maximum Pay Per Share

This approach is almost the same as the Pay Per Share approach. However, this method caps the payments to what the pool earned.

Equalized Shared Maximum Pay Per Share

This approach is similar to Shared Maximum Pay Per Share but the payments are distributed to all members of the pool.

Recent Shared Maximum Pay Per Share

This approach is similar to Shared Maximum Pay Per Share. However, this method gives priority to the most recent miners.

Capped Pay Per Share With Recent Backpay

This approach makes use of a reward system based on maximum pay per share for miners who found blocks, but the pay is capped so that the pool won't go bankrupt.

Bitcoin Pooled Mining

This approach provides more weight to the most recent shares than to older shares and effectively reduces cheating by switching pools within a round.

Pay On Target

This approach is the same as the pay per share method. However, this gives more weight to the difficulty of work by the miner.

Score

This approach provides an equitable reward that gives more weight to later shares instead of older shares. Each share has a score based on the time it was submitted.

Eligius

This approach combines pay per share and Bitcoin pooled mining. Payouts are made by the pool immediately as miners deliver their proof of work. Rewards are equitably distributed to all shares. However, payouts are made only if the miner earns a minimum of 0.67108864. If the miner earns less than that, his earnings will be rolled over to the next round.

Triplemining

This approach connects pools that are of medium size and doesn't charge fees. It redistributes 1% of each found block so each miner's share grows faster.

Categories of Bitcoin Mining Hardware

Before deciding what computer hardware to use for mining, it is important to consider hash rate and energy consumption. Hash rate is the rate at which the computer hardware can perform mathematical computations. It is measured in terahashes, gigahashes, and megahashes per second. If the hash rate is high, there's a better chance that a transaction block will be solved. Energy consumption, on the other hand, should be considered because it translates to expenses the miner has to pay in order to mine Bitcoins.

CPU/GPU Mining

In essence, the ordinary computer can be used to mine Bitcoins but the hardware is extremely slow. The hash rate can be increased by adding a graphics card to the desktop computer. Nvidia and ATI are very good suppliers of GPUs. One advantage of using GPUs is that they can be used in mining other cryptocurrencies. However, Bitcoin miners don't use GPUs anymore because the difficulty of mining Bitcoin has greatly increased so that it now requires the use of ASIC power to mine Bitcoins.

FPGA Mining

A Field Programmable Gate Array is a circuit that allows a manufacturer of mining hardware to purchase chips and customize the circuit prior to including it to the equipment. Because it is specifically designed for mining, this FPGA offers improved performance as compared to CPUs/GPUs.

ASIC Mining

The Applied Specific Integrated Circuit is customized for Bitcoin mining. It uses less electricity but operates at the fastest speeds. However, this circuit is expensive and takes a lot of time to manufacture.

Calculating Mining Profitability

Before deciding to commit to mine Bitcoins, an individual must compute for the project's profitability first. There are online mining profitability calculators where an individual has to input parameters like present Bitcoin price, power consumption, hash rate, and equipment cost for him to know the payback rate of his investment. Network difficulty is also an important parameter. ASIC devices increase the network difficulty.

Chapter 13: Litecoin Mining

Litecoin is the second most popular cryptocurrency, next to Bitcoin. It is cheaper than Bitcoin, but it is gaining ground in terms of market support. Also, it is easier to enter Litecoin mining because it isn't as popular as Bitcoin.

Required Software and Accounts

Litecoin Wallet - This program acts as a repository for Litecoins. It can be downloaded from the official Litecoin website. Deposits and transfers are possible through this electronic wallet. To secure the Litecoin wallet, it must be encrypted. Regular backup is also necessary so that the Litecoins can be retrieved in case the computer crashes.

Pooled Mining Account - There are various Litecoin mining pools online that a new miner can join. It is best to research a mining pool before one decides to be a member of it. Reliability is an important factor in choosing a Litecoin mining pool.

Stratum Proxy - This offers mining efficiency and is lightweight. It also auto-connects to any mining client.

Litecoin Miner Software - CGMiner, GUIMiner, and Reaper are just a few examples. The GUIMiner -Scrypt is another option. It has pre-defined graphics settings.

Secure Router - It is important not to connect the desktop computer to the modem directly. A router must be used, but a firewall must be enabled because there are hackers that can attack the Litecoin operations.

Litecoin Mining Hardware

The mining industry for Litecoins is not as developed as that for Bitcoins. Though ASICs computers can help miners mine for Litecoins, they are very difficult to buy. Since the Proof of Work program that Litecoin uses is different from the one used by Bitcoin, users who mine Bitcoins cannot mine Litecoins. For example, some of the hardware that people use to mine Bitcoins is not available for Litecoin. Graphic cards are the best alternative hardware for mining Litecoins. However, they do not bring much in terms of profit. Any miner who is keen on mining Litecoins should reconsider such a move. A better option would be to mine Bitcoins and then convert them to Litecoins.

How to Mine Litecoins

Step #1: Download the Litecoin wallet

Create a Litecoin wallet. Litecoin-Qt is available for download from Litecoin.org. It must be installed on a computer. It is important to note that exchanges and online wallets should not be used to store Litecoins. A user should always make sure that their coins are stored securely in their wallet. Once the wallet has been downloaded and installed, a backup should be created. Run the program and let the wallet sync. This process may take a couple of hours but ultimately generates the user's unique Litecoin address.

Step #2: Get the Litecoin Mining Hardware

In order to mine Litecoins, a user needs to have proper GPUs. Though theoretically CPUs can also be used to mine Litecoins, this is no longer recommended. The difficulty of mining Litecoins has become so high, and with the extremely low hash rate of CPUs, it has become impossible for a miner to earn any meaningful returns this way. The best option is to use a graphics card, for example, AMD or NVIDIA cards. Since AMD cards tend to mine Litecoins faster, they are highly recommended.

Step #3: Download the software and Drivers

Download the chosen miner software and install on the desktop computer as well. Litecoins can be mined using either CGminer or GUIminer. If a user has chosen to buy an AMD graphics card, then the appropriate drivers would be the latest version of AMD Catalyst Software Suite drivers.

Step #4: Join mining pool.

In choosing a pool, a lot of individuals consider fees, rewards, and size. In general, payouts from a large pool are frequent but a miner may get less Litecoins. A small pool usually pays more Litecoins but less frequently. To join a pool, the individual must create an account on the pool's website. It is also important to add worker accounts per miner software. For the pool setup, it is necessary for the individual to determine the right server settings.

The Difference Between CPU and GPU Mining

The central processing unit (CPU) is an integral part of a desktop computer that ensures the software's performance. It directs every part of the computer by following the software's program code. Today, most computers possess multi-core CPUs while some have many CPUs inside of them. The central processing unit is removable and can be plugged in the main circuit board of the computer. It is usually found below the fan while there are some models that are water-cooled.

On the other hand, the graphics processing unit (GPU) is tasked with video rendering in the computer. It helps render visual effects and 3D graphics. In most cases, a server may have no or limited GPU. A lot of computers use integrated graphics processor, a cheaper, slower, and less power consuming kind of GPU. A graphics processing unit is often needed for video editing or gaming. GPUs are designed for repetitive tasks like trying various hashes repeatedly, which is the main procedure behind Litecoin mining. As such, GPU mining is faster than CPU mining.

How Profitable is Litecoin Mining?

The speed of mining Litecoins is determined by luck, present network difficulty, and hash rate. An individual can control only the hash rate by opting to buy graphics processing units and setting them up for optimum performance. The revenue a person obtains from Litecoin mining is reduced by hardware outlay and electricity costs.

This means that there are only certain narrow conditions under which Litecoin mining becomes profitable. People today can no longer earn Litecoins using CPUs and GPUs. Powerful special mining computers called ASICs are now available for mining Litecoins at a much faster rate and with greater efficiency. This has resulted in the phasing out of the old hardware. The problem with CPUs and GPUs is that the cost of mining using such hardware is much greater than the returns. They are simply not worth the effort.

Any miner who wants to buy hardware for mining Litecoins needs to first consider a few factors:

1. The amount of power being consumed. It won't make sense for your electricity bill to exceed your Litecoin profit.
2. The difficulty of the network. With an increase in the number and speed of miners in the network, mining profitability will decrease. It is, therefore, crucial that a realistic prediction is made regarding the future evolution of mining difficulty.
3. The low resale value of ASIC hardware. Though ASICs are very efficient in mining Litecoins, they aren't much good for anything else. Therefore, they cannot be sold or reused for another purpose.
4. Delays in delivering preordered mining hardware. There is no point in having your mining equipment delivered months after ordering.

There are many profitability calculators available online. In most cases, the calculator will ask for the hash rate, the average electricity cost, and the estimated power usage of the mining setup. The resulting value is then multiplied with the current price of Litecoin and reduced by the power cost per day. The difference is the gross profit per day.

Litecoin Mining Difficulty

This is considered one of Litecoin's most significant features. The Litecoin mining difficulty is an algorithm that varies depending on the total hashing power within the network. It is also worth noting that mining difficulty changes for every 2,016 blocks mined in order to ensure that confirmation time remains at 150 seconds. If the price of Litecoins goes up, there would be a great increase in mining activity. As more and more Litecoin miners join the mining network, the difficulty rises. This means that the profit per day may be reduced drastically.

Advantages of Litecoin over bitcoin

1. Unlike Bitcoin, which has a set production limit of 21 million coins, Litecoin has a higher limit of 84 million coins. This means that Litecoins will outnumber Bitcoins by 4 to 1. Litecoins will end up being cheaper, more widely circulated, and easier to obtain.
2. Litecoin mining requires a powerful graphics card instead of just a fast processing chip. This means that more people are able to mine Litecoins by simply using their gaming PCs. Bitcoin mining, on the other hand, is usually done by the few people who can afford to buy special computers with extremely fast chips.
3. It takes a mere 2.5 minutes to confirm a transaction, unlike Bitcoin which takes 4X longer. Purchases can be performed faster with Litecoins.

Disadvantages of Litecoins

1. Most merchants are yet to accept Litecoins as payment. However, this situation is changing every day.

2. Litecoins are not as well-known worldwide as Bitcoins are.

Chapter 14: Dogecoin Mining

To mine Dogecoin, an individual needs an AMD/ATI video card. High-end video cards often have faster processing times compared to cheaper ones. Even without the graphics card, it is still possible to get into Dogecoin mining. However, CPU mining is much slower.

How to Mine Dogecoins

Step #1: Download the Dogecoin Wallet.

A person must obtain a Dogecoin wallet from dogecoin.com and install it on his computer. It is important to temporarily disable any antivirus software, as it will automatically delete the Dogecoin wallet installer. Protect the wallet from hackers and viruses by encrypting the wallet. Once the Dogecoin wallet file is installed and extracted, it has to be synced with the Dogecoin network. This is to enable the user to send and receive funds. This process sometimes takes hours. Once the wallet has been installed, the directory where the Dogecoin wallet is installed must be excluded from the antivirus software's scans. It should be noted that the syncing process does not interfere with a user's ability to start mining.

Step #2: Download the software

The next step is to download and install the GUI miner for Dogecoins. The miner should be tested once it has been installed on the computer. The miner must be set to run even when the system is idle.

The person can expect to get paid between 4 to 8 hours after mining has started.

Step #3: Join a Mining Pool

Mining coins as a group is always more beneficial because users will be able to find coins in less time. A good place to look for Dogecoin mining pools is Dogepool.com. Mining as an individual can be very frustrating as a miner may mine a block for days and still fail to get any rewards. Choose a credible pool that is reliable and won't go offline for no good reason.

Dogecoin also uses the same mining algorithm used by Litecoin. Any Litecoin mining program should also work with Dogecoin mining. However, Dogecoin rewards differ because blocks are discovered every minute with the following rewards:

0 to 1,000,000 Dogecoins for block 1 to 100,000
0 to 500,000 Dogecoins for block 100,001 to 200,000
0 to 250,000 Dogecoins for block 200,001 to 300,000
0 to 125,000 Dogecoins for block 300,001 to 400,000
0 to 62,500 Dogecoins for block 400,001 to 500,000
0 to 31,250 Dogecoins for block 500,001 to 600,000
0 to 10,000 Dogecoins for blocks greater than 600,000

Dogecoin Mining Hardware

Dogecoin mining is not as developed as Bitcoin mining. Bitcoins Proof of Work algorithm can be solved using ASICs computers, and though these computers can also be used when mining Dogecoin, they are not easy to purchase. Dogecoins do not have specialized mining hardware of their own. Graphics cards are the only option, though they will not earn a user much reward. Another possibility for Dogecoin miners is to simply use Bitcoin mining hardware and then convert their Bitcoins into Dogecoins.

Why Join A Dogecoin Digging Pool

To join a mining pool, the person must register with his chosen pool. He needs to setup a username and password for the CPU miner he intends to use. If there are different computers that will mine Dogecoins, it is best to create different usernames and passwords. It is not advisable to mine Dogecoins alone because it is difficult and slow to search blocks.

CPU Miner Setup

Usually, a Dogecoin client includes a CPU miner, but different mining software can also be used. There are different mining software versions, depending on the operating system. As such, the individual must use the correct miner for his computer.

How Profitable is Dogecoin Mining?

Because Dogecoin mining uses the CPU functionalities instead of GPU, it isn't as profitable as one may expect. However, Dogecoin can be a good way to learn about cryptocurrencies. Besides, it's fun to learn cryptocurrency mining. Dogecoin rewards are also greater than Bitcoin and Litecoin rewards. Thus, a person can earn more Dogecoins even when he's just using his computer's CPU.

Advantages of Dogecoin Mining

1. Unlike its two more popular cousins, Dogecoin is not limited in terms of supply. Dogecoins will continue to be added to the network annually at a stable rate.

2. There are more Dogecoins in circulation today than Bitcoins, thus making each Dogecoin of lesser value. However, this makes Dogecoins easier to use since consumers can buy goods/services with a couple of Dogecoins rather than using a fraction of a Bitcoin.

Disadvantages of Dogecoins

1. Dogecoins are not yet widely accepted as payment compared to Bitcoins.
2. Dogecoins are not as popular globally as Bitcoins.

Chapter 15: Bitcoin Security Tips and Safety Features

It is critical that every Bitcoin user or miner be conscious of security. This is because most individuals are used to a fiat currency system, where a large financial institution is left with the full responsibility of protecting people's money. If there is a problem, there is always someone to fix it. Most people aren't used to taking full responsibility for the security of their money, which is why a lot of mistakes are made when handling Bitcoins. There is nobody to call to fix a person's own mistake. With Bitcoin, caring for security is everything.

Basic Security Rules

There are some steps an individual can take to prevent loss of Bitcoins. The most common ways that an individual can lose their Bitcoins are through theft, user error, or technical failure. The rules described below are the best ways to secure a Bitcoin account:

1. Enable the account's 2-Factor Authentication
The 2-Factor Authentication prevents anyone from stealing a user's Bitcoins using their password alone. Attackers have ways of acquiring Bitcoin users passwords, so individuals should go to their account management area to set up a 2-Factor Authentication.

2. Maintain direct control of private keys
An individual should always store their Bitcoins in a wallet that they have total control over. Wallets contain both public and private keys, with the public key representing the Bitcoin address. Controlling the wallet means controlling the Bitcoins within. If a user buys Bitcoins

from an exchange and delays withdrawing them, they will lose their funds if the exchange gets hacked. This is also true if an individual stores their Bitcoins in an online wallet. Withdraw all Bitcoins from exchanges and only leave a few that may need to be traded in the near future. Users should avoid using online wallets unless the amount being stored is under $100.

3. Ensure regular backup of the Bitcoin wallet
A Bitcoin user must regularly back up their important data. It is the best way to protect money against loss of a wallet. It is recommended that users confirm which files to back up from the developer of the wallet software. Keep three backups on two different devices (for example USB and Hard Drive), and give a friend one backup to store for you.

Bitcoin Nodes

A node is any computer that is connected to the Bitcoin network. These nodes are responsible for making sure that all Bitcoin rules are enforced. There are full nodes and lightweight nodes, but it is the full nodes that keep the network more secure. The responsibility of a full node is to download each block and transaction made, and confirm if they adhere to Bitcoin's main consensus rules. These rules include:

1. A block is only allowed to create a set amount of Bitcoins.
2. Every transaction must have the right signatures.
3. Blocks and transactions need to be in the required data format.
4. A transaction output can never be double-spent in one block chain.
Any transaction or block that tries to violate these rules is totally rejected by a node, regardless of whether other nodes validate it. This

feature of the Bitcoin network makes sure that the right thing is always done no matter what. A full node does not fully rely on the miner, thus making it extremely difficult for someone to change or bring down Bitcoin.

As a user, having a full node is the best way to use Bitcoin with full confidence. Full nodes ensure that the network is secure and are presently the most private means of using Bitcoin. They are immune to the numerous attacks that lightweight wallets suffer from and prevent attackers from learning about a person's private Bitcoin addresses.

It is in every Bitcoin user's best interest to use full nodes instead of lightweight nodes, as this will ensure the survival of the Bitcoin economy. Full nodes will always impose the consensus rules regardless of the situation, but lightweight nodes will not. Lightweight nodes tend to blindly follow whatever the majority of the mining power tells it. Lightweight nodes can even be tricked into approving blocks or transactions that are not valid. It is only full nodes that provide maximum security and privacy for users within the Bitcoin network.

It is recommended that users run the Bitcoin Core wallet in order to run a full node. Users need to avoid a lightweight client such as MultiBit unless it is configured to connect entirely to an individual's full node.

Chapter 16: Important Cryptocurrency Websites

Since cryptocurrencies became popular, more and more digital currencies have popped up. It becomes difficult for an individual to keep track of the developments for each cryptocurrency. Even information about Bitcoin has become disparate. It's good to know that there are quite a number of websites that can truly help an individual's search for the right information.

The Alternate Cryptocurrencies Subforum - Found in Bitcointalk forums, this section is dedicated to all other cryptocurrencies. Almost all of the new digital currencies are announced in this subforum.

Coinchoose - This website offers information on thirty cryptocurrencies and focuses on data involving miners. Network hashpower, price, reward, difficulty, and mining algorithm are found in this site. It also provides mining probability of a cryptocurrency in relation to Bitcoin. Coinchoose offers information that will help an individual choose which cryptocurrency to mine.

CrypTrader - Through this application, an individual can link his accounts to Vircurex, Bter, BTC-E, and MtGox so that he can instantly trade on different exchanges in just one single page.

Quandl Bitcoin Markets - This site provides statistics related to Bitcoins like Bitcoin transactions, blockchain size, average block size, and Bitcoin prices.

Ripple Charts - This website offers different charts for different currency markets. It is also the best source for information about the price of Ripple.

CryptCoin Monitor - This is an Android app to help individuals monitor their mining pool accounts.

Cryptsy - This is an exchange where at least 30 alternative cryptocurrencies can be traded for Bitcoins.

Cryptocoincharts - This website provides charts for at least 70 cryptocurrencies.

Cryptocoin Explorer - This is similar to Bitcoin's block explorer but is dedicated to 15 alternative cryptocurrencies.

Chapter 17: Taxation Issues on Cryptocurrencies

Tax havens hide taxpayers' earnings from the government by providing small tax environments that aren't subject to activities that require information exchange. In the United States of America, at most $70 billion of yearly revenues are lost to tax havens. An estimated $255 billion of annual revenues are lost globally. Because of this, countries have been arguing for taxing offshore accounts.

In 2010, the Foreign Accounts Tax Compliance Act was enacted in the United States of America. This law aims to compel financial institutions in other countries to identify US citizens who have accounts with them and report them to the Internal Revenue Service. If an institution doesn't file a report to the IRS, it will be subjected to a 30% gross tax on some payments received from sources in the US. This means the foreign financial institution which has major business transactions in the USA can either pay the hefty tax to the country or breach its home country's bank secrecy laws by submitting the required report to the IRS.

With this new development, it is possible for these tax evaders to shift to cryptocurrencies instead of the traditional tax havens. Although cryptocurrencies like Bitcoin are used in legitimate transactions, they can also be used in illegal activities like tax evasion. Like the usual tax havens, cryptocurrencies aren't controlled by the government in which they thrive. Therefore, they aren't taxed at source. Cryptocurrencies also offer user anonymity. More importantly, Bitcoin and other cryptocurrencies aren't dependent on financial intermediaries.

Therefore, cryptocurrency transactions aren't covered by the Foreign Accounts Tax Compliance Act.

Cryptocurrency transactions, however, may not be significant to tax evasion because the market for such transactions is really small. However, if the market continuously grows, tax evasion may become a problem. Studies have shown that Bitcoin is being used as a savings account by some of its owners. Bitcoin wallets have become repositories and Bitcoins, which go into the e-wallets, aren't used for transactions anymore. Earnings from these cryptocurrency wallets aren't reported to taxing authorities. Furthermore, some research has shown that a lot of Bitcoin users utilize patterns like "fork and merge," where huge holdings of Bitcoins are distributed to different accounts by just one owner. Money launderers and tax evaders can use this strategy to hide their holdings from authorities. There are also some individuals who openly admit to using cryptocurrencies as a way to circumvent taxation duties.

Currently, governments are aware of the challenges these cryptocurrencies present in terms of regulation. However, these same governments fail to fully comprehend the taxation dilemmas such cryptocurrencies cause. There was a recommendation in the 2013 GAO Report to inform taxpayers of tax reporting requirements for virtual currency transactions. However, this doesn't address the tax collection difficulty these cryptocurrencies present. Earnings from cryptocurrency transactions must be taxed, but informing taxpayers about it doesn't solve tax evasion. Taxpayers who really want to evade their taxation duties can willfully withhold the information about their cryptocurrency transactions.

It is important for governments to draft mechanisms that will permit tax authorities to search for funds in cryptocurrency accounts. Because cryptocurrency transactions aren't that widespread yet, authorities haven't shown any serious action. However, if cryptocurrencies are expected to stay, these governments must seriously create an action plan to address the issue.

Current mechanisms to curtail tax evasion aren't applicable to cryptocurrencies. There is no exchange of information agreement because cryptocurrencies aren't sanctioned by any government. Although statistical analysis can be used to identify owners of cryptocurrencies, it can't address the problem systematically. The innovation that brought about these cryptocurrencies requires innovative policymaking. It requires a full inquiry to come up with all possible solutions.

Germany has taken the initial steps to tax cryptocurrencies as capital assets. This means that cryptocurrency holders in that country must report revenues when they sell their cryptocurrencies in the same way they report revenues from the sale of other financial assets. However, this strategy holds true for transactions at the point of exchange. It doesn't tackle unreported and unexchanged cryptocurrencies, which remain in the possession of the owners.

Conclusion

I hope this book was able to help you to understand Bitcoin and cryptocurrencies so that you can take advantage of the many earning opportunities such digital currencies offer. Learning about these innovative electronic currencies can be your stepping stone towards greater financial freedom.

The next step is to decide which of the many cryptocurrencies you'd like to try mining or investing in.

Finally, if you enjoyed this book, please take the time to share your thoughts and post a review on Amazon. It'd be greatly appreciated!

Finally, we would like to ask you to give a short, honest, and unbiased review of this book.

Please & Thank you!

Instant Access to Free Book Package!

As a thank you for the purchase of this book, I want to offer you some more material. We collaborate with multiple other authors specializing in various fields. We have best-selling, master writers in history, biographies, DIY projects, home improvement, arts & crafts and much more! **We make a promise to you to deliver at least 4 books a week in different genres, a value of $20-30, for FREE!**

All you need to do is sign up your email here at http://nextstopsuccess.net/freebooks/ to join our Book Club. You will get weekly notification for more free books, courtesy of the First Class Book Club.

As a special thank you, we don't want you to wait until next week for these 4 free books. We want to give you 4 **RIGHT NOW**.

Here's what you will be getting:

- A fitness book called "BOSU Workout Routine Made Easy!"
- A book on Jim Rohn, a master life coach: "The Best of Jim Rohn: Lessons for Life Changing Success"
- A detailed biography on Conan O'Brien, a favorite late night TV show host.
- A World War 2 Best Selling box set (2 books in 1!): "The Third Reich: Nazi Rise & Fall + World War 2: The Untold Secrets of Nazi Germany".

To get instant access to this free ebook package (a value of $25), and weekly free material, all you need to do is click the link below:

http://nextstopsuccess.net/freebooks/

Add us on Facebook: First Class Book Club

CPSIA information can be obtained
at www.ICGtesting.com
Printed in the USA
LVOW13s1104270617

539532LV00005B/975/P